SWINDON
& THE GWR

SWINDON
& THE GWR

Felicity Ball & Tim Bryan

Frontispiece: Great Western Railway Castle Class engine No.5087 *Tintern Abbey* in action on the Swindon Works Locomotive Test Plant. Situated in the Erecting Shop, this equipment allowed the company to run locomotives at high speed under test conditions without the need to venture onto the main line.

First published in 2003 by Tempus Publishing
Reprinted 2006

Reprinted in 2008 by
The History Press
The Mill, Brimscombe Port,
Stroud, Gloucestershire, GL5 2QG
www.thehistorypress.co.uk

© Felicity Ball & Tim Bryan, 2003

The rights of Felicity Ball & Tim Bryan to be identified as the Authors of this work has been asserted in accordance with the Copyrights, Designs and Patents Act 1988.

All rights reserved. No part of this book may be reprinted or reproduced or utilised in any form or by any electronic, mechanical or other means, now known or hereafter invented, including photocopying and recording, or in any information storage or retrieval system, without the permission in writing from the Publishers.

British Library Cataloguing in Publication Data.
A catalogue record for this book is available from the British Library.

ISBN 978 0 7524 2801 7

Typesetting and origination by
Tempus Publishing Limited.
Printed and bound in Great Britain.

Contents

	Acknowledgements	6
	Introduction	7
one	Swindon Works in the Steam Era	9
two	Swindon Works at War	45
three	Swindon Works: the Diesel Era	61
four	Great Western Swindon: Outside the Works	81
five	Swindon Station and Locomotive Shed	101
six	Swindon Products: Some GWR Locomotives	111
seven	Great Western Preserved	117
eight	Great Western Miscellany	123

Acknowledgements

The authors are grateful to a number of people who helped in the compilation of this volume. Thanks are particularly due to David Hyde, Brian Earl, and the many other volunteers who have assisted in the sorting and identification of our collection. Assistance has also come from John Fleetwood, John Harrod, Jack Hayward, Roy Nash, Alf Neate, John Plaister, Jim Sheppard, Fred Vellender, John Walter and the GWR Engineering Society who have helped identify some of the pictures included here.

We are grateful too for the support of our partners on the Swindon Works site, including Jeremy Baker of Carillion Development, Franco Muccini and staff at the Great Western Designer Outlet Village, and Keith Falconer at the English Heritage.

We would also like to acknowledge the support of our colleagues at the Swindon Reference Library, and the National Railway Museum at York. A number of 'official' pictures are reproduced courtesy of the National Railway Museum.

The authors would also like to thank the rest of the team at STEAM: Museum of the Great Western Railway for their help and support during the compilation of this collection.

Whilst every effort has been made to determine the sources of pictures reproduced in this volume, some are unidentified, and some many years old. We apologise to anyone we may have missed, and will ensure that any omissions will be rectified in future editions.

Finally, we owe a great debt to the photographers, railway enthusiasts, railway staff and local people who have collected and saved much of the material reproduced in this book for posterity. Local historians such as the late Alan Peck, and the enthusiast Jim Russell, whose pictures are collected here, have done much to keep the memory of Swindon's past alive and relevant to future generations.

Introduction

Swindon & the GWR, which follows *Great Western Swindon*, further builds upon the story and history of the Great Western Railway through a selection of photographs which offer a fascinating insight into the workshops of the Locomotive, Carriage & Wagon Works at Swindon, and the lives of those who worked within them. For almost 150 years, Swindon was the manufacturing centre of the GWR, where locomotives and rolling stock were built and maintained in the vast workshops that made up 'The Works' complex. Swindon itself, a small backwater until it was chosen by Daniel Gooch as the ideal site for the GWR to base its workshops, developed and grew as a railway town, where the influence of the GWR was evident in every aspect of its residents' lives.

Those readers who have visited the former Great Western Works site at Swindon in the last few years will not fail to have noticed the stark comparison between the images reproduced in this book and the site as it is today. The workshops, which were once home to heavy industry, are now occupied by representatives of the leisure and heritage industry, including McArthur Glen Designer Outlet Centre, English Heritage and The National Trust. However, the historic significance of the site and the story of the GWR in Swindon have not been lost, but are preserved and told at STEAM: Museum of the Great Western Railway, which occupies a building on the site which was once the 'R' Machine & Turning Shop.

STEAM developed from what was previously Swindon's GWR Museum, which was based in Faringdon Road, and opened in July 2000. The collections and archives from the old museum are now given justice in a large, imaginatively redeveloped building. It is from the collections at STEAM that this second selection of images is taken. A number of significant photographic collections have been recently received into collections at STEAM, containing previously unseen material, some of which is published in this volume for the first time. Included are images taken from the Alan Peck Collection, and from the Jim Russell Collection, both of which include a treasure trove of albums documenting the history and development of Swindon

Works. In drawing together material from a variety of different collections, it is hoped that this selection of images will give the reader a unique and unreserved insight into the industry that once dominated the town of Swindon.

To find out more about the collections held at STEAM, visit the museum website at www.swindon.gov.uk/steam

The famous tunnel entrance to Swindon Works pictured in June 1966. The doors are firmly shut and one of the watchmen stands to attention waiting to greet any visitors. The picture was taken to illustrate both the new sign and the new uniform issued to the watchmen.

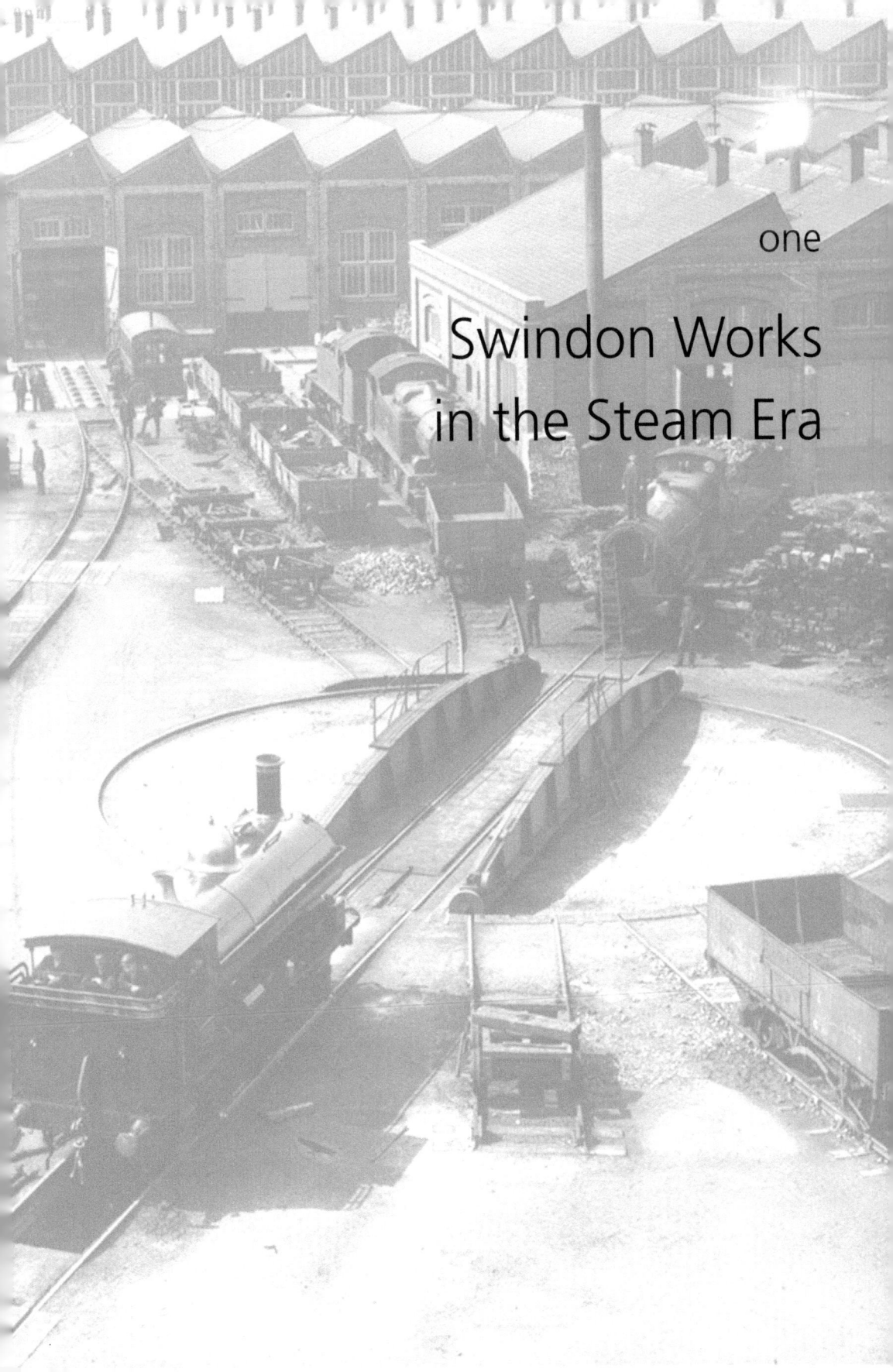

one

Swindon Works in the Steam Era

Swindon was transformed by the coming of the GWR in 1843. The sleepy market town was changed into a large industrial settlement. Although the Railway Works was initially a small development, employing around 1,000 men, by the First World War the site covered over 300 acres and almost 12,000 staff were employed building locomotives, carriages and wagons for the company. The pictures in this chapter chronicle the work which took place in the works from the nineteenth century until the late 1950s, when the construction of steam locomotives finally ceased at Swindon; by this date, the Great Western had ceased to exist, following the nationalisation of the railways in 1948. The end of steam was symbolically marked by the construction at the works of 2-10-0 locomotive *Evening Star*, which was the last steam locomotive to be built by British Railways.

An aerial view of the Railway Works and Swindon Junction Station dating from the 1930s. In total the workshops covered and area of over 323 acres at its greatest extent, and although a good deal of the Carriage & Wagon Works is visible, particularly to the right of this photograph, much of the Locomotive Works remains out of sight beyond the General Offices, which can be seen to the right of the main line at the top of the picture.

Opposite below: Until the Second World War, most women employed by the GWR at Swindon worked in the offices, and this photograph taken on 17 August 1929 shows the 'Comptometer' Office. Comptometers were early adding machines and the clerks can be seen working their way through the large piles of paperwork. Unlike many of the workshops elsewhere in the factory, the offices were lit by electricity, as can be seen by the rather grand fittings which decorate the ceiling.

Right: The three-storey General Offices complex was reached by the subway which ran from the Tunnel Entrance shown at the beginning of the book, and housed almost all the office staff needed to run the huge railway works. On the top floor were two drawing offices: one for the Locomotive Department, the other dealing with Carriage & Wagon and miscellaneous work including Dock Gates, Locomotive Sheds and other items dealt with by Swindon. This 1932 view of the entrance also shows the drawing board used by Brunel, which was displayed there for many years. The board is now exhibited at the STEAM Museum.

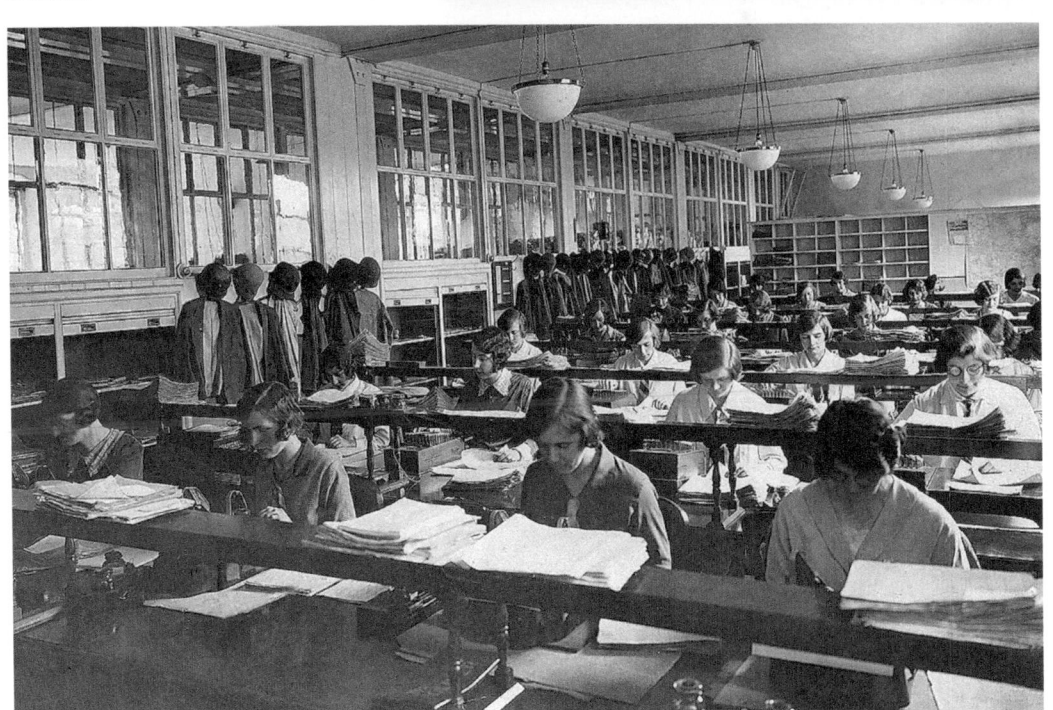

Above: In 1929, part of Brunel's original works was demolished to allow more modern workshops to be built. The atmospheric photograph shows the Engine Shed, close to the original 1843 Engine House, just prior to its demolition. The original wooden Brunel roof can be clearly seen, and, to the right, the more modern girders of the 'B' Shed, used for the maintenance of tank locomotives and tenders, is visible. A small group of workmen are making a poor effort at hiding from the camera behind the workbench in the centre of the picture.

Opposite above: An early view of office staff from the works. This sepia photograph is not dated, but was probably taken in the early 1890s. Of particular note is the fact that the clerk seated in the middle of the front row is none other than F.W. Hawksworth, who would eventually become Chief Mechanical Engineer of the GWR in 1941. A carpet has been thoughtfully provided for the most junior member of staff who is sitting on the floor.

Opposite below: Virtually all workshops within the complex had their own 'shop office' where foremen and other clerical and supervisory staff worked. This undated postcard shows the 'R' (Machine) Shop offices. Fittingly, these offices have survived as part of the STEAM Museum, and still house administrative staff.

One has to be full of admiration for the stamina of the intrepid photographer who dragged his plate camera up the stairs of St Mark's Church tower to take this 1860 view of the Works, probably the earliest photographic record of Swindon Works. The picture shows the building now occupied by the STEAM Museum, originally built in 1846 as a Machine & Turning Shop. Beyond the chimney of the Engine House, which was used to power the machines in the building, open country can be seen; it was soon to be covered in houses as the Works and town grew. In the foreground, one of the many entrances to the Works can be seen, although at this time men crossed the railway by the board level-crossing running across the tracks, rather than a subway.

Over a century later, much has changed! This 1982 photograph, also taken from St Mark's Church illustrates how much the Works and the town had expanded. The 1846 Machine & Turning Shop has been considerably altered and expanded. The courtyard visible in the 1860 view, on the right-hand side of the picture, was roofed over in the 1860s when the Carriage & Wagon Works closed. The building, which had remained a Machine Shop since its construction, was converted into a Wheel Shop, a role it assumed until the Works closed in 1986.

The Iron (J1) Foundry produced hundreds of tons of ferrous castings each year. This photograph, taken in 1951, shows molten metal being poured into a large moulding box used to produce locomotive cylinders for British Railways Class 4 engines. The mould is large, and as a result has been placed in a hole in the foundry floor. Smaller moulding boxes can be seen in the foreground. Castings of this size could take up to three days to cool before movement. The foreman wearing a Trilby hat is Charlie Webb; to his right, holding a rod, is Bill Garrett. Operating the ladle are Harry Titcombe (left) and Ernie Cave (right).

Two postcard views of the Foundry. The one on the left, dating from 1931, shows the production of a casting for a tunnel arch. Because of the sheer size of the component, no pattern was produced; instead the casting was created in the floor of the Foundry itself using special moulding sand, without the need for a moulding box. The view on the right shows the finished product, suspended from one of the cranes in the workshop after cooling.

Opposite above: The original 'O' Tool Shop as pictured by the Swindon postcard photographer, William Hooper. The Tool Room was responsible for the production of many of the precision tools, gauges and other specialist equipment used in the Works.

Opposite below: The relocated 'O' Shop, situated next door to the Boiler Shop. There is much detail in this 1950s picture: as well as the usual machinery and tooling (in the centre left of the picture), below the shop office can be seen the workshop check board, used to record workers presence before the introduction of 'clocking in' clocks. Above the board is the original GWR drop-dial clock, and to the left, the workshop first aid box. This location is now the west entrance to the Designer Outlet Village.

17

Above: A drawing office print of a publicity photograph, probably taken for the *Great Western Railway* magazine, the company's staff journal. The GWR bandsman at work in one of the Swindon Machine Shops is not named in this photograph, which is dated 25 March 1938.

Right This photograph shows an impressive stack of steam-locomotive cylinders, which have been bored out, faced and fitted with studs in one of the Machine Shops in the Works. Health and safety was of great importance and the notice hanging from the wall above the finished cylinders in this 1951 view warns staff to replace safety guards on machines when in use.

Above: Despite the fireworks display created by this Butt Welding Machine, the workman in charge appears only to have a leather apron for protection. The photograph was taken on 14 September 1951.

Right: The L2, or Tank Shop, was where the locomotive water tanks and tenders were constructed, and is now part of the Designer Outlet Village. Here, workmen are welding the drag box of a British Railways standard steam locomotive.

Above: Boiler construction and repairs were carried out in two locations at Swindon Works. As well as the Boiler Shop situated close to the Foundry, work also took place in a section of the 'AV' Erecting Shop. This photograph, taken in December 1962, shows Boiler No.5856, originally built in 1947, awaiting repair.

Left: A snapshot taken by one of the staff from the 'A' Shop in 1961, showing the hydraulic riveter crane, which allowed boilers to be hung vertically from the roof. This made riveting much easier. The names of the group inside and outside the boiler are not recorded. The roof of the workshop was raised to enable King Class locomotive boilers to be worked on.

Opposite: A clearer view of the equipment pictured in the previous photograph, taken some twenty-three years earlier in 1938. The enormous crane hook used to hold the boiler can be seen at the top of the picture, as can the hydraulic riveting equipment.

A striking view of one of the journal lathes used in the AW (Wheel) Shop.

The lathe pictured in this view of the Wheel Shop was used for a very specialist task: that of turning the wheel crank pins onto which locomotive connecting rods and valve gear were attached. Although the picture was taken over six years after the end of the Second World War, a sign for an air-raid shelter can still be seen hanging from the girders on the left-hand side of the picture.

The Wheel Shop, already mentioned, can be seen in the background of this early view of the 'A' Erecting Shop, dating from around 1920. The Erecting Shop was the location where the final assembly of new and repaired locomotives took place. The white asbestos that was used to lag boilers can be clearly seen on the boilers of Star Class locomotives in the centre of this picture.

There is much to see in this 1951 view of the Erecting Shop. In the foreground a gang is at work fitting a combined reversing shaft and quadrant link bracket to a BR Class 4 4-6-0, whilst on the left-hand side of the picture, work on riveting the frames of an engine has paused while the picture is being taken. Finally, a painter is hard at work in the cladding of 4-6-0 6862 *Derwent Grange*.

Although there is no date on the postcard reproduced here, it is likely that the photographer took this picture during the construction of the 5600 0-6-2 class of locomotives, built at Swindon Works between 1924 and 1928.

Above: As well as standard gauge locomotives. Swindon also maintained the locomotives used on the narrow gauge Vale of Rheidol Railway which ran from Aberystwyth to Devils Bridge. The 2-6-2 tank No.8 is seen outside the 'A' Shop in May 1962.

Opposite below: The enormous size of the Erecting Shop presented difficulties in terms of moving large locomotives, but this photograph illustrates two methods employed by the railway to overcome this. On the left of the picture, a Castle Class locomotive No.5020 *Trematon Castle* is being lifted by one of two 100-ton cranes capable of lifting completed locomotives. In the centre of the picture, BR 2-6-0 No.77000 is being moved on one of the traversing tables used throughout the Works.

This group of 'A' and 'B' Shop foremen, photographed in October 1946, are sitting in front of an extremely grubby 4-6-0 No.5975, *Rolleston Hall*, which has probably received an intermediate overhaul. The economies and difficulties experienced as a result of post-war austerity meant that it was some time before pre-war standards could be achieved. The group consisted of: (standing) J. Gregory, P. Jarvis, S. Abrams, C. Keefe, S. Earp, (seated) J. Owen, S.A. Millard, W. Bullock.

Opposite above: The finishing touches are added to BR Class 4 4-6-0 No.75001 at the Works on 26 June 1951.

Opposite below: Standing outside the 'A' Shop after an overhaul in May 1962, 4-6-0 No.6925 *Hackness Hall*, originally built at Swindon in 1941, waits to be reunited with its tender before being put back into traffic.

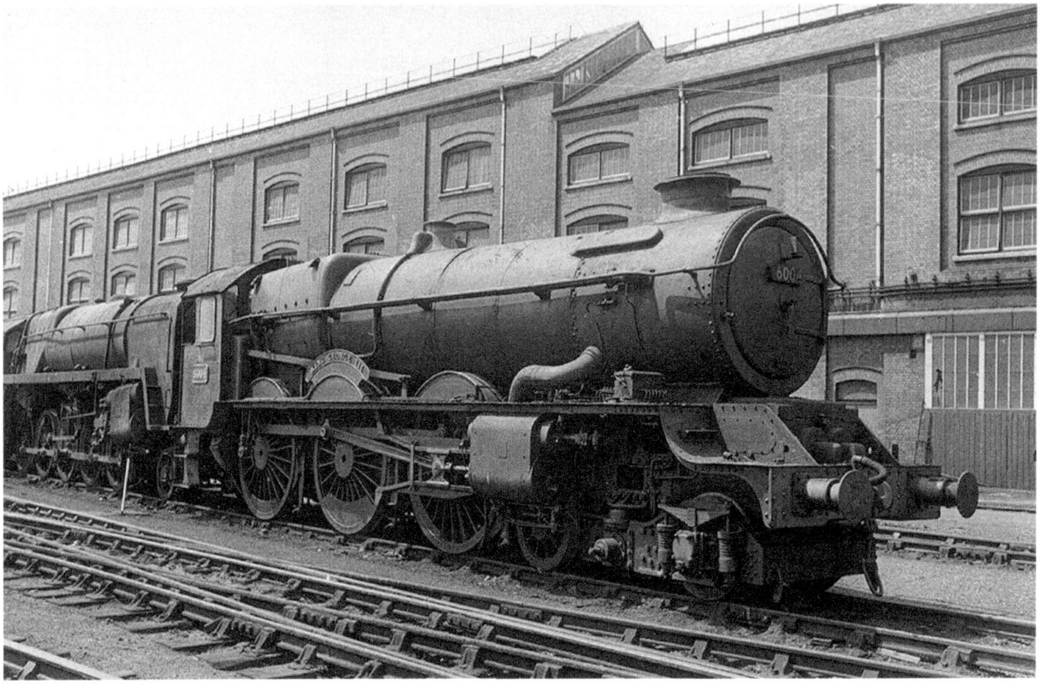

The locomotive No.4082 *Windsor Castle* shown prior to its use on the funeral train of His Majesty King George V on 26 January 1936. Members of the GWR Engineering Society have been able to identify some of the staff, although those standing on the engine itself remain anonymous. The bottom row from left to right are: Stan Millard (Chief Fitter/Foreman 'A 'Shop), Herbert Price (fitter), unidentified, Mr Bezzant (Vacuum Fitting Gang), three further unidentified staff, Jim Owen (Assistant Chief Foreman 'A' Shop), and Walter Dew (Fitter/Foreman 'A' Shop).

Opposite above: The sidings outside the Works also played host to a more sombre sight: that of once great locomotives awaiting their fate at the hands of the breakers' torch. In May 1961 GWR express locomotive No.6004, *King George III*, is pictured next to a BR 9F 2-10-0, withdrawn and ready for scrapping.

Opposite below: West of the 'A' Shop was an even larger group of withdrawn locomotives stored in Concentration Yard. This May 1962 photograph taken by enthusiast and railway historian Jim Russell shows the cab of No.4990 *Clifton Hall*, and the forlorn sight of No.4094 *Dynevor Castle*, originally built at the Works in 1926.

Above: On 20 June 1951 the driver of the 100-ton overhead crane looks on from above as staff make final preparations before the Class 4 BR Standard locomotive is lowered down on to its bogie.

Opposite below: The line of locomotives shown in this photograph illustrates the end of the broad gauge era in 1892. Brunel's great experiment to utilise an entirely new track gauge of 7ft ¼in instead of the preferred 4ft 8½in used by his rivals, cost the Great Western dear, not least at Swindon, where the company had to purchase extra land west of Rodbourne Road to store the locomotives and rolling stock that was made obsolete by the final conversion of the broad gauge in that year. Although some locomotives had been designed to be converted, many of those pictured here were cut up for scrap. In the distance the chimneys of the foundry furnaces can be clearly seen, and the tower of St Mark's Church is visible above the trees of the GWR Park.

The photographer has chosen the top of the Pattern Shop as his vantage point for this 1908 photograph. Looking west from Rodbourne Road, there are many details to interest an historian, enthusiast or modeller. Four people on the Saddle Tank locomotive No.1642, built at Swindon in 1880, are posing for the picture and one intrepid apprentice is standing on the top of the smoke box of an unidentified 2-4-0. In the background, outside the then new 'A' Erecting Shop is an enormous line of tenders and locomotives. On the left, beyond the timber store, is Newburn, the home of the Locomotive Superintendent G.J. Churchward.

Left: There were two sawmills within the Carriage & Wagon Works at Swindon. This photograph, taken in October 1950, illustrates the use of a Robinson Horizontal Band Saw, which was being used to cut a very large piece of wood in to a more manageable size.

Below: At a rough count, there must be upwards of 150 staff visible in this 1924 photograph of the Carriage Finishing Shop. Although there were a large number of roof lights, each bench was also equipped with gas lights. With the close proximity of so much combustible material, it was no wonder that fire precautions were very strict. Note also the woodblock floor, made up of blocks of scrap timber from redundant rail vehicles.

Above: The Carriage Body Shop was the equivalent of the 'A' Erecting Shop on the locomotive side, where component parts from various workshops were combined to produce the finished carriages. This 1946 photograph shows construction of a Hawksworth coach underway in No.4 Shop.

Right: An unidentified Engineers Inspection Coach being insulated with fibreglass. This picture dates from 1948; later British Railways carriages and diesel multiple units were lagged with the much more toxic blue asbestos, which has had serious consequences to ex-railway staff in health terms in recent years.

Above: A striking view of a third-class corridor coach built at Swindon Works in 1949. Although still constructed using the conventional timber framing for the body, this example was fitted with an experimental aluminium under-frame.

Opposite: The massive flywheel of this Bliss Electric Press towers over the young apprentice using it in this photograph taken on 22 June 1936. The machine was located in the Stamping Shop.

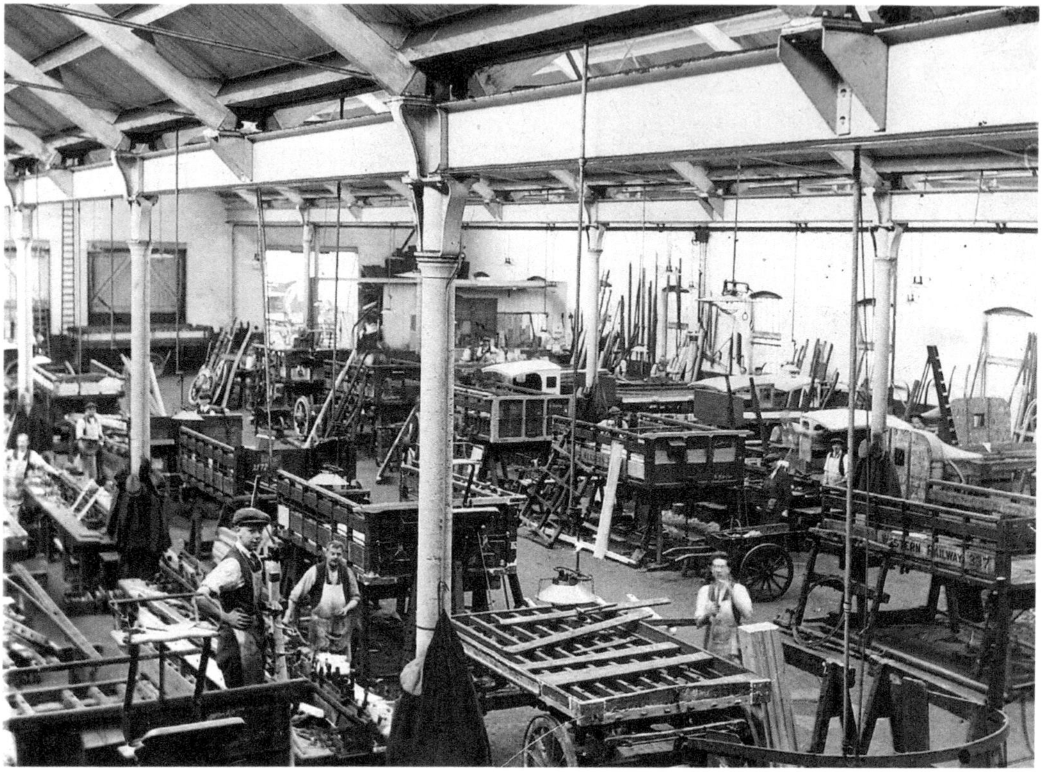
WESTERN RAILWAY

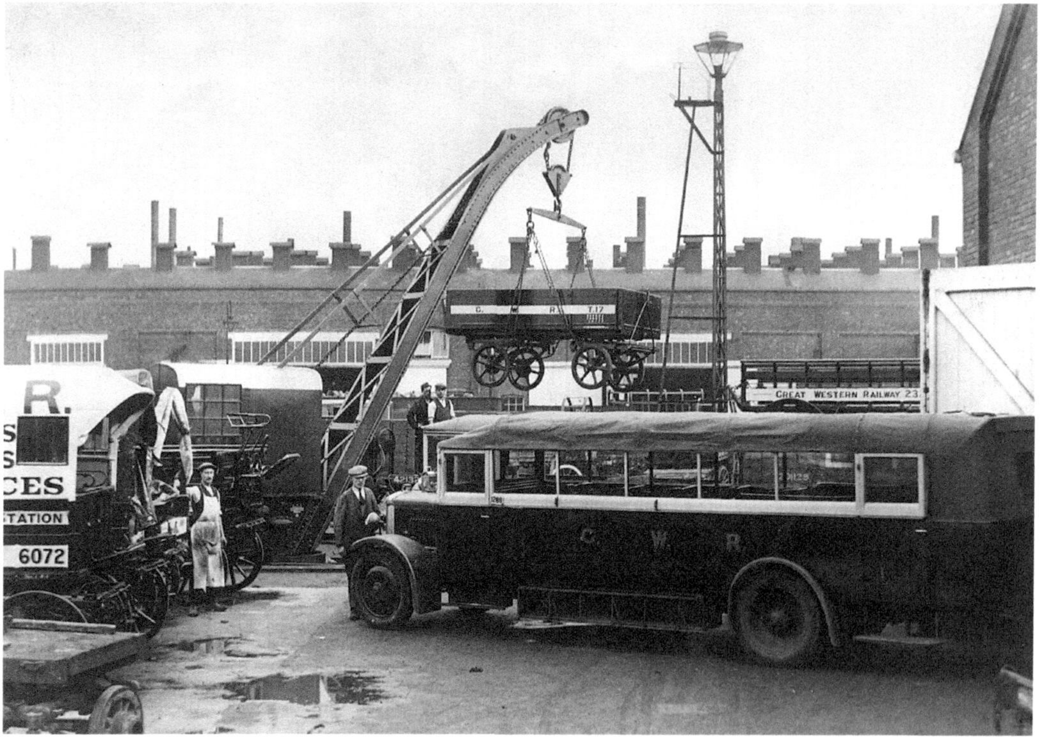
CES
STATION
6072
GREAT WESTERN RAILWAY
G W R

Two female staff from the Carriage & Wagon Department engaged in the manufacture of the nets used in carriage luggage racks, their day clothes clearly visible under their company-issue overalls.

Opposite above: The scene inside the Road Wagon Shop in the 1920s. Although the workshop also built new vehicles, almost all the wagons in this view appear to be part of the Great Western's large fleet, which are in the shop for repair or overhaul. Horse-drawn wagons predominate, although the cabs of at least two motor vehicles can be seen peeping above the middle row of vans.

Opposite below: The scene outside the Road Wagon Shop. A selection of Great Western road vehicles are displayed for the photographer, the two most prominent being the bus, which was a Guy FBB chassis fitted with a Buckingham 'all weather' type body. Vehicles such as these were used for 'land cruises' operated by the Great Western in places like Dartmoor and North Wales. The other prominent feature is the 2-ton 'Carrimore' trailer with fixed sides, which is suspended from the crane.

Left: One of the many traversing tables which were used in both the Locomotive and Carriage Works. This example was situated in the latter works, and was manufactured by the Ipswich firm of Ransome & Rapier. Unlike some used at Swindon, it had a cabin to house the operator. This picture shows Bert Reeves standing close to the capstan used to pull the carriage on and off the table, watched by Chargeman Jack Warwick.

Below: Chargehand Fred Farncombe outside No.15 (Bogie) Shop of the Carriage Works, standing next to the prototype B4 bogie developed at Swindon, and used on British Railways carriages.

The clutter inside the Carpenters Shop is evident in this 1953 view of what was the 'Utility' Shop of the department. Staff employed here were asked to turn their hand to a huge variety of jobs, some of which can be seen in the picture. The young carpenter in the foreground is working on a standard GWR-issue platform trolley, whilst, as well as the new stepladders to his left, various other wheelbarrows can be seen in the background.

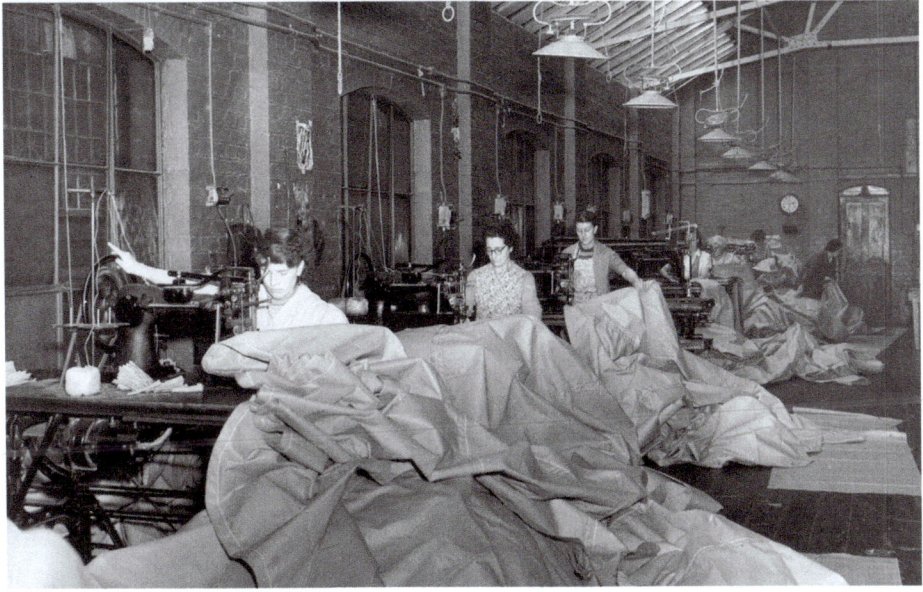

Despite the fact that this picture was taken in 1960, the staff working in the Sewing Room still appear only to have gas lighting, even though their sewing machines are electrically powered. Quite what the ladies seen here were sewing together is, unfortunately, not recorded on the picture.

Above: Wagon Shop staff photographed in 1924. The two office boys seen here look extremely young!

Left: The War Memorial in No.7 (Finishing & Polishing) Shop as photographed in 1947. Following the Second World War, two names had been added to the Great War total of nine who had fallen in conflict. Unlike many other memorials, which have survived and are now on public display, the whereabouts of this example is not known.

Opposite above: The Oil Works & Store was located on the eastern side of the Carriage & Wagon Works close to the Laundry in Whitehouse Road. This undated view shows oil drums being unloaded prior to being loaded into storage tanks.

A photograph taken in the No.15 (Bogie) Shop which emphasises the family tradition in Swindon Works. Shown in the picture is Chargeman Fred Farncombe, who had started his life in the Works in 1909, and his son, thirty-six-year-old Kenneth, who was Shop Foreman at the time the picture was taken. Fred, also pictured on page 38, was in charge of fourteen men whose job it was to build the bogies used on carriages and diesel multiple units.

42

Opposite top: A retirement gathering for Mr H.F. Smith, who had been the Foreman of No.3 (Press) Shop. Leaving the Works after over fifty years service, he was presented with the traditional chiming clock by Mr F.R. Hitchens, Chief Foreman. Ken Farncombe, seen in the previous picture, can be seen to the right of Mr Hitchens.

Opposite below: The test of a new forklift truck at the Sawmill at the west end of the Works in May 1954. The authors are not sure that the huge pile of timber on the forks would have actually fitted into the wagon seen here!

Above: Although not in a very good condition, this photograph taken by a member of staff in 1959 of the Central Boiler Station is worthy of inclusion since it clearly illustrates the massive proportions of the chimneys, then being reduced in size. Some idea of the scale of these chimneys may be gained from the fact that each individual section was formerly the boiler barrel of a Dean Goods locomotive.

Left: A photograph taken by the Drawing Office in 1951 to illustrate a new device to safely drop the large and heavy cast-iron vacuum cylinder from the underside of the body of a carriage.

Although not strictly part of either the Locomotive or Carriage & Wagon Works, the Gas Works on the site was a large and important part of the operation at Swindon. This picture, taken in 1956 as part of plans for a new Points & Crossing Shop nearby, shows the scale of the Gas Works. One of the two gasholders in the picture is still in operation, although the scene here has been dramatically altered by a dual carriageway which slices through what was the Works site.

two

Swindon Works at War

Although the Works had played an important role in the war effort during the First World War, like many other railway workshops during the Second World War the skills and equipment contained at Swindon made it invaluable to the War Department.

The Great Western were called on to manufacture all manner of equipment for the war effort, including ambulance trains, landing craft, tanks, gun-mountings and other items, as well as huge quantities of munitions. There is not space here to list all the smaller jobs tackled by staff, however it is not surprising that the day-to-day work of maintaining the locomotive and rolling stock fleet suffered. The Works employed several thousand women during the war years, replacing men called up for military service, and pictures of the invaluable work done by them are seen here.

A photograph taken in March 1941 from the roof of the Carriage Paint Shop looking towards the premises of Compton, Sons & Webb, the factory close to the Works where many of the uniforms worn by GWR staff were manufactured. The two arrows in the picture indicate the position of two anti-aircraft posts situated on the roof of that building.

Above: The intrepid photographer has clambered up onto the roof of the 'A' Erecting Shop in this view taken on 29 March 1941. Looking west, this view shows a number of locomotives awaiting repair outside the workshop, whilst a long goods train trundles past the Works travelling east. In the background, the long camouflaged building is the Newburn Carriage Shed, built on the site of Newburn House, the former residence of Locomotive Superintendent G.J. Churchward, seen elsewhere in this volume.

Right: The 1,000lb bomb in this picture dwarfs the workman sanding beside it. This photograph was taken to illustrate bombs with and without vanes, in the 'X' Shop. This workshop was used to manufacture track crossings and points before the war.

Above left: Quite what the significance of the hammer carried by the workman in this 1941 view of 2,000lb and 4,000lb bombs is, is a mystery, although it does also illustrate very clearly the blackout conditions which staff worked under during the war, since windows and roof lights were painted over.

Above right: A photograph taken in December 1940 illustrating testing taking place on the suspension lug fixed to the casing of a 250lb bomb manufactured in the 'X' Shop.

Three female staff at work on an Aldous Campbell press, which was used to insert base plates and copper bands on to 25-pounder shells. This picture was one of a series taken in the 24F Shop in the Carriage & Wagon Works where a production line was set up for the Ministry of Supply to manufacture shells.

A further photograph of 24F Shop taken in February 1942 showing the production line for 25-pounder shells.

Three months after the picture of the production line was taken, the photographer returned to 24F Shop to record the scene in the Shell Inspection Department. The artificial light under which much war work took place is clearly evident.

A scene in No.5 Shop on 20 August 1941. Summer sun is streaming through the windows, the blackout blinds having been rolled up, and a welcome change from artificial light. Staff are winding the coils and armatures for 230-volt alternators used in radio location equipment. Not surprisingly, work such as this was considered highly secret at the time.

Opposite above: A very posed photograph taken outside the 'L2' Tank & Tender Shop in 1941, showing a 400lb bomb casing fitted with rollers being brought into the building. The two staff seen here illustrate the fact that many people approaching or past retirement stayed on at work during the dark days of the 1939-1945 conflict, to help the war effort. The space seen behind the men is now the children's playground in the Great Western Designer Outlet Shopping Centre.

Opposite below: One of the many female staff employed in the Works during the war, hard at work on a lathe in the 'B' Shop, turning the outside of a shell. The worker in this June 1942 picture has no overalls to protect her, although she is wearing a net to prevent her hair becoming tangled in the machinery.

An even more secret task carried out by the Works during the Second World War was the construction of the superstructure of these miniature submarines for the Admiralty. This photograph, taken in No.7 Shop of the Carriage Works, shows the wooden pattern made initially in 1942.

A further view taken almost a year later in June 1943 of the same workshop, showing the finished product. The photograph also illustrates some of the precautions taken to keep the work secret, with both high wooden screens and canvas sheeting erected to hide the submarines from prying eyes.

Despite all the work being done for the War Department, day-to-day tasks still continued in the factory. This photograph, taken in the Tinsmiths Shop in the Locomotive Works, shows female staff soldering signal lamps.

The expertise contained within the Railway Works in the construction of locomotive tanks and tenders made it an obvious place to manufacture equipment such as landing craft and tanks. This photograph was one of a series taken on the day that this completed vessel was loaded onto a road vehicle in June 1942. The landing craft is being moved by a GWR Pannier Tank locomotive on a small rail trolley to a position where the large crane in the background can lift it onto the lorry. The width of the landing craft made it too big to be moved on the railway.

Taken outside the building now occupied by the STEAM Museum, then called the 'R' Machine Shop, this 1940 photograph shows various parts of 'Rackham' clutch and final drive parts for 25-ton tanks being loaded onto a rail wagon. They were then taken to a LMS Works where the final assembly of tanks took place.

In peacetime, the Road Wagon Shop in the Carriage & Wagon Works illustrated elsewhere in this book was called on to carry out repair work on the large fleet of road vehicles used by the GWR. As the war progressed, they also had to repair vehicles damaged in air raids. This lorry, photographed there in December 1940, had been damaged in an air raid at Bristol the previous month.

Another disturbing photograph showing the effects of bombing on the Great Western fleet. Carriage 4447, which the image records had been damaged at West Kirby near Liverpool, was pictured outside the Carriage Works in February 1941.

The J1 Foundry building is the scene for a picture showing the No.3 Company of the Swindon Battalion of the Home Guard on parade in February 1941. After a hard day at work in the factory, many men volunteered for Home Guard duty, protecting what was a very strategic location on the railway.

A GWR 0-6-0 Pannier Tank locomotive stands in the background, whistling in salute, and the Works General Offices provide the backdrop for the passing out parade of the GWR Home Guard in 1945. From the large puddles evident in the picture it is either raining or has rained relatively recently, and the Home Guard are all wearing their standard issue greatcoats.

As already mentioned in this chapter, despite all the war work being done, day-to-day work continued. The demands of the War Department did, however, restrict both new building and locomotive overhauls, through shortages of staff, materials and the poor working conditions suffered by staff, as illustrated in this 1943 picture of a King Class locomotive in the 'A' Shop.

Above left: Taken close to the turntable near the Pattern Shop of the Railway Works, this photograph, taken in June 1944, shows driver Selwood of Swindon Shed on the footplate of Castle Class locomotive *Earl of Powis*. The photograph also shows one of the blackout precautions used by the company on its locomotives. The cab window has been removed and replaced with the riveted sheet seen here. The blackout was completed by a tarpaulin, which was fixed between the cab roof and the tender, which cut out much of the light emitted from the locomotive firebox, but was hated by crews, particularly in the summer months when it made being on the footplate like being in a sauna.

Above right: The front end of one of the 2-8-0 American S160 locomotives used on the Great Western and other main line railways in Britain until taken to the Continent after D-Day. The Works plate of this ALCO example reads September 1942. It is not surprising that staff at the Railway Works, raised on the clean lines of Star, Castle and King Class locomotives, found the ugly – if workmanlike – design of these engines hard to come to terms with! The photograph was taken at the west end of Swindon Works in December 1942.

Opposite above: Swindon Works suffered from few air raids during the war, a number of pictures of some of the more serious attacks appeared in the first volume of this book. This rather fuzzy image shows some of the staff of No.24 Shop inspecting one of the bomb craters resulting from a raid on Swindon on 27 July 1942.

Opposite below: The dangers of fire in the Carriage & Wagon Works were remarked upon earlier in this volume, and this photograph shows the aftermath of a fire in the Polishing Shop and Carpenters Shop in May 1945. A workman is perched perilously on the roof of the building, presumably making an inspection of the damage done, whilst a group of schoolboys are peering into the wagon in front of the workshop.

NEG. WDO/116
PHOTO'D. 27.7.42

59

The ubiquitous Dean Goods locomotives had already seen service in one world war when this photograph was taken in December 1939. The robust design of the class meant that it was an ideal candidate for use by the War Department, whose number and initials are carried by this locomotive.

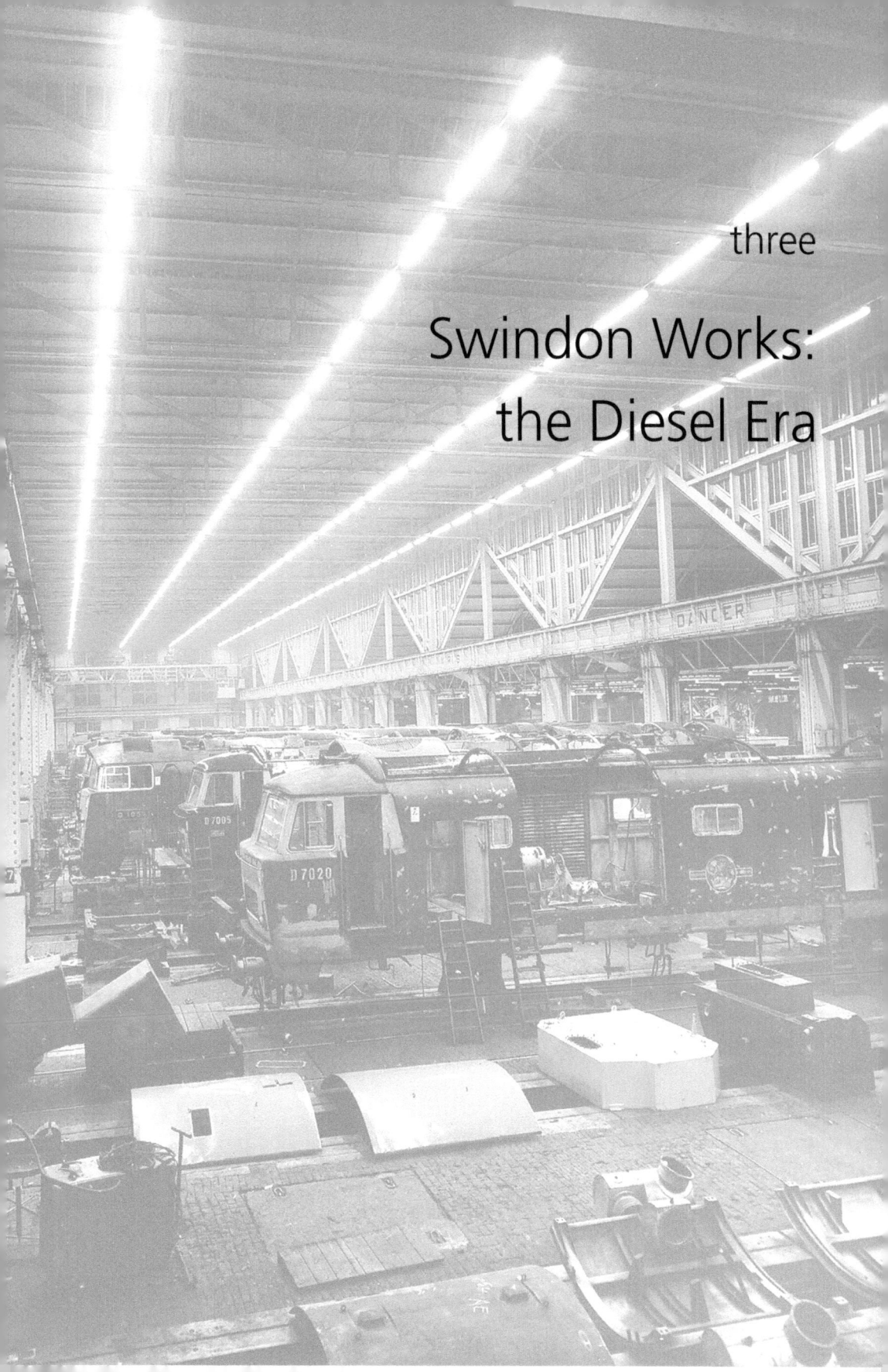

three

Swindon Works: the Diesel Era

It is hard to believe that the Railway Works at Swindon have now been closed for over seventeen years. Although the title of this chapter may suggest an element of modernity, many of the pictures reproduced here were taken well over forty years ago. The coming of diesel traction meant that changes in the way the Works operated were inevitable; new equipment and working practices ensured that the process of evolution started by Brunel in 1843 continued. The most dramatic changes occurred in the 1960s when a radical reorganisation of the Works took place, a result of the end of steam and a reduction in workload. Alan Peck, author of the definitive history of the Works, did much of the planning for this reorganisation, and many of these pictures illustrate the move from steam to diesel at Swindon. Despite all the work done then, the fortunes of the Works were in gradual decline, and despite the efforts of Harry Roberts, Works Manager in the 1970s, the end finally came for the Works in 1986.

The Locomotive Stores offices at Swindon seen in June 1962, showing the modern equipment then installed and presenting a contrast with the offices seen in the previous chapter. Despite the new desks and office furniture, an old-style GWR drop-dial clock is still in evidence on the wall in the background. Also visible in the picture are the double-glazed windows installed in GWR days to reduce the noise from the factory outside.

Double-glazed windows similar to those visible in the previous picture are also evident in this portrait of Jim Ridout, of the Carriage & Wagon Drawing Office, in June 1966.

In the next office, taken on the same day, was Dorothy Boulter hard at work on what was an old GWR desk, despite the relatively modern typewriter she is using.

Rodbourne Road, photographed in May 1964 before the onset of modernisation work which would see a new canteen being built on the site, occupied by the wagons seen on the left-hand side of the picture. The old P1 Shop in the centre, formerly used as a Boiler Steaming Shop, was to be converted into a Transport Garage. In addition, a new entrance to the Works, eventually known as the 'West Gate', was constructed next to the P1 Shop.

The scene further down Rodbourne Road at the junction with Church Place, showing a new sign at the Park Lane entrance and also a new sign which had been fixed to the side of the Pattern Shop. The picture was taken on a grey day in January 1968.

One of the 'Work in Progress' photographs taken during the reorganisation of the Railway Works which took place after the closure of the Carriage & Wagon Works in 1961. Taken from the roof of the Pattern Shop, the picture shows the new Works canteen nearing completion, surrounded by much evidence of building work still under construction.

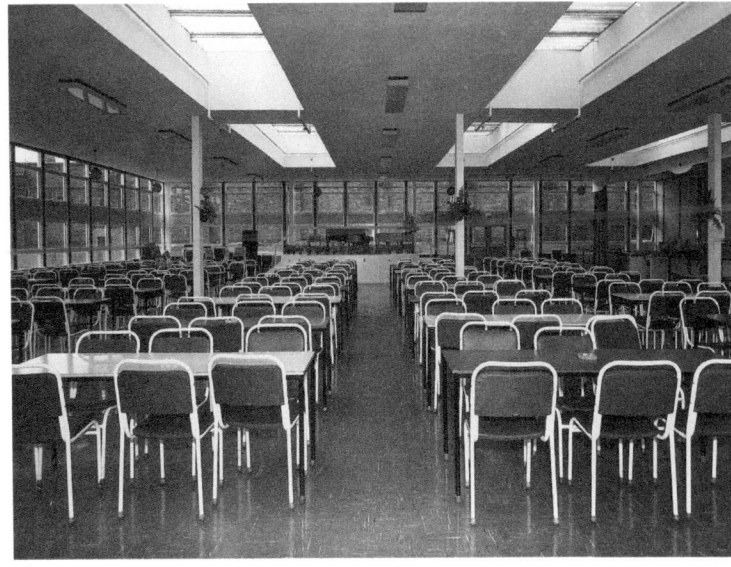

The interior of the new Works canteen, as seen in September 1966. The stage has been set up for a concert, complete with a grand piano!

Considerable modernisation work was carried out in the square surrounded by the 'G' Shop, the 'B' Shed and the Locomotive Works Manager's Office. This view, taken in September 1966, shows the considerable modifications made to 'B' Shed, seen on the left of the picture, to convert it into a location where Diesel Multiple Unit's could be overhauled. To gain access into the workshop, a new traversing table was installed, although it was not completely new, having been moved over from the old Carriage & Wagon Works before closure. In the background, behind the Works Manager's Office, is the 'R' Shop, the building now part of the STEAM Museum.

Opposite above: A view looking towards the old Foundry building, which is visible in the distance, with the old Blacksmiths Shop on the left and the 1874 Boiler Shop complex on the right. Visitors to the site today would see a much-changed site, since this is now the entrance to the Food Court of the Outlet Village. The area between the buildings is now glazed over and also contains GWR 4-6-0 locomotive *Hagley Hall* on loan from the Severn Valley Railway.

Opposite below: The scene in the Brass Foundry in 1966 is a distinct contrast to that shown in the earlier view of the Iron Foundry reproduced in chapter one. The workshop has more of a production line feel to it, and the concrete floors and fluorescent lighting were much different to the gas-lit GWR era. The picture was taken to illustrate the installation of more modern lighting.

The interior of what had been known as the 'R' Machine & Turning Shop was also modified dramatically. All the old machines were removed, the woodblock floor was lifted, and the building was turned into a modern Wheel Shop. This photograph shows a number of the wheel lathes installed there. Under the boarding to the left of the lathes was a conveyor belt, which was used to remove the metal swarf created during the turning of wheels, journals and axles. The shop offices can be seen in the background, accessed by a wooden staircase.

Opposite above: The movement of wheels around No.20 Shop was effected by tracks let into the new concrete floor. This image taken by local photographer L. Maylott illustrates one of the hydraulic rams used to lift and turn wheels allowing them to be easily positioned without the need for cranes.

Opposite below: By modern standards this machine is now probably seen as fairly primitive, but in the 1960s it was a world away from much of the equipment used in GWR days. Behind the control panel, a wheel gauge, used to check the profile of wheel tyres, can be seen hanging from a bracket on the wall. Even with more modern machinery in use, the dirt and grime generated in the Railway Works is still very apparent in this picture!

With the change from steam to diesel, new facilities were created to enable diesel locomotives and their engines to be maintained. Taken in May 1966, this view shows another part of the Diesel Engine Repair Shop shown opposite. This small room was used to repair and maintain fuel injection pumps.

A very clean and tidy 'G' Stores in the Carriage & Wagon Department, photographed in December 1958.

One of the most striking transformations during the modernisation process of the 1960s was that which took place in the old J1 Foundry building. With the end of steam locomotive construction, the need for two foundries was removed, and so the large building was converted into a vast diesel engine repair workshop, which dealt with engines from all manner of both Swindon-built and other locomotives and diesel multiple units. On a production line basis, engines were stripped down, cleaned, repaired and re-assembled; this view taken from about halfway down the workshop shows the large overhead cranes which had been retained from the old building, and men hard at work on the production line.

The 'A' Erecting Shop in September 1966, with a selection of Swindon-built diesel hydraulic locomotives in evidence. Two Hymek Class engines are in the foreground, whilst behind them No.1054 *Western Governor* is under repair.

Right: An earlier view of the 'A' Shop, taken by the Drawing Office as part of a series of pictures of the inspection of the experimental Metro Vickers Gas Turbine Locomotive No.18100 at the Works; one of the bogies of the locomotive is seen in the foreground. One of two locomotives purchased by the Great Western just prior to Nationalisation of the railways. Although very powerful, neither locomotive was completely reliable, and both spent much time in the Works under repair!

Below: The building which had been the Locomotive Boiler Shop in the steam era was converted into a Wagon and Container repair facility during the modernisation process. Here, in this 1967 picture, staff are unloading a wagon from the electric traversing table into the workshop.

Above: Work being carried out on a British Railways restaurant car in the 'A' Shop in February 1981.

Left: A photograph of the man who had much to do with the reorganisation of the Railway Works in the 1960s, Alan Peck. He later went on to research and write the definitive history of Swindon Works, and much of his collection is now in the care of the STEAM Museum. Alan, who died in 2001, is standing next to the old Sand Furnace chimney prior to its demolition on 7 July 1966.

Opposite above: The scene a few minutes after the previous picture of Alan Peck was taken. Staff from the Pattern Shop on the right of the picture can be seen watching the chimney fall to the ground.

An illustration that however modern railways become, there will always be dirty and unpleasant jobs which need to be done by railway staff. This picture, taken in November 1966, shows the underside of a Warship Class diesel hydraulic locomotive being cleaned.

Although taken in the 1980s, this photograph could have been taken a century before! The workshop portrayed is the Spring Shop, and the men shown here are working to produce a leaf spring, using techniques which have varied little for many years. More leaves can be seen awaiting heating next to the furnace in the background.

The huge variety of tasks undertaken by the Works throughout the years has been remarked on many times, and Swindon photographer Roy Nash has illustrated this fact very clearly in this picture of the Rope Shop. Here wire ropes, hawsers and chains were manufactured and overhauled. Next door, in the Chain Test House, the strength and safety of chains and ropes could also be checked. The hydraulic press shown here is being used to press a metal collar onto the wire rope.

Although the tradition of apprentice training was strong at Swindon, with skills being passed on from generation to generation through the apprenticeship process, it was not until the 1960s that Swindon had its own Training School. This view shows the Machine Shop of the school, which was situated close to the Works in Newburn Crescent.

An obviously posed publicity picture showing one of the staff passing on the benefit of his experience to apprentices. The hairstyles seem to indicate that the picture dates from the early 1960s.

Apprentices D. Findlay and B. Stone stand outside the British Railways Sports Ground with the Swindon Apprentice Shield in June 1961.

The 0-6-0 diesel hydraulic shunter No.9500 pictured in 1967. Built with a centre cab for better visibility, these locomotives were intended for use on light goods or shunting duties, but proved not to be powerful enough for this task. Nicknamed 'Teddy Bears' by trainspotters, a number have been preserved and are in use on heritage railways.

Truly the last locomotives built at Swindon. A series of these 0-8-0 shunters were built at the Works for Kenyan Railways. Shown on the traverser outside the 'A' Shop, No.4731 is posed before being made ready for export.

The first of the D800 Warship Class diesel hydraulic locomotives, *Sir Brian Robertson*. Although this picture is dated September 1967, this particular locomotive was built in August 1958.

The caption on this photograph, taken outside the 'A' Shop in 1973, remarks that this engine, Western Class locomotive No.1023 *Western Fusilier*, was the last to be repaired at Swindon Works. This was not entirely true, since various other diesel shunters and multiple units continued to be worked on until closure in 1986.

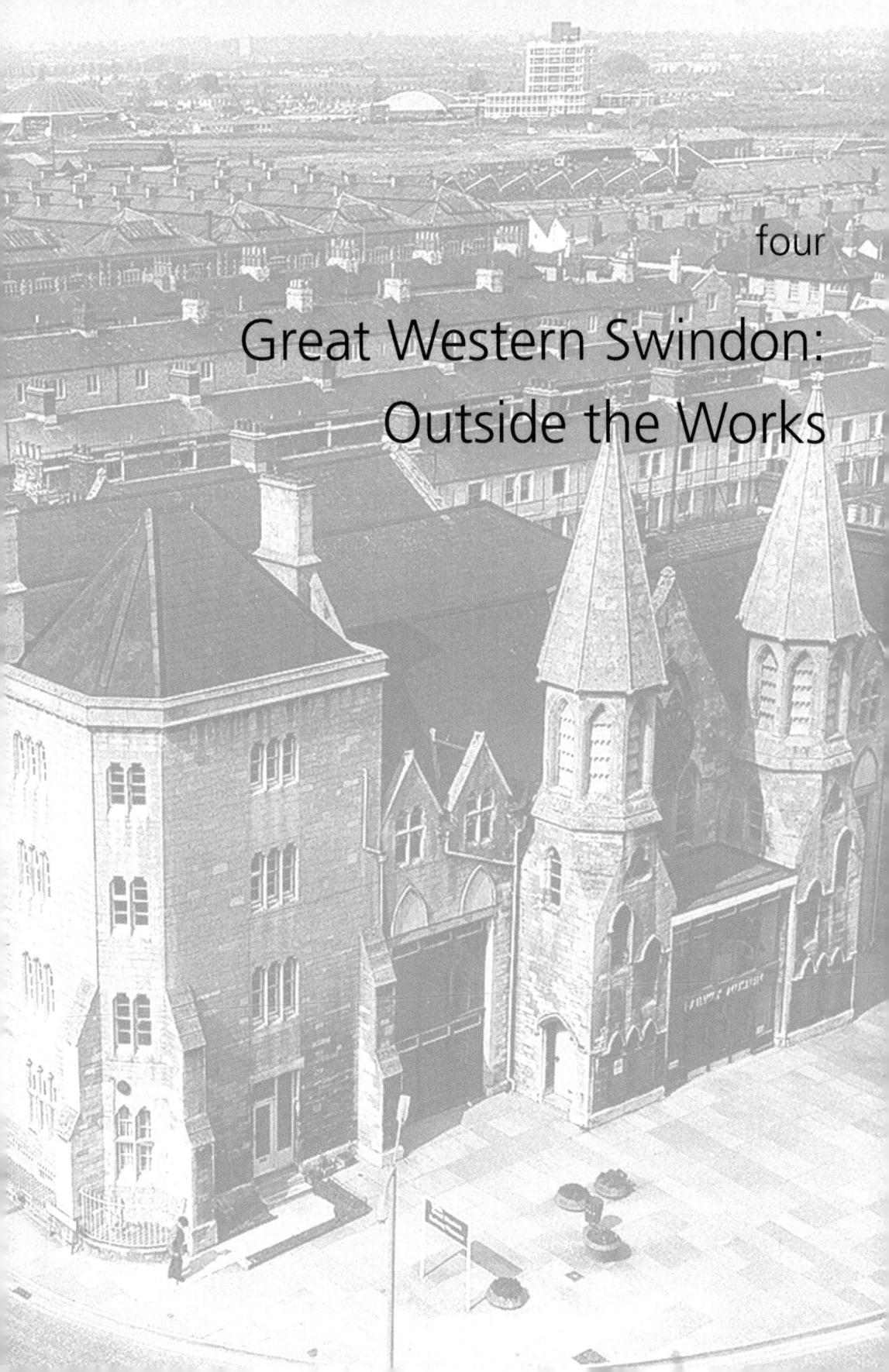

four

Great Western Swindon:
Outside the Works

For those employed within Swindon Works, the GWR was not only a job but a way of life. 'New Swindon' grew up as a direct result of the GWR's decision to base its Locomotive, Carriage & Wagon Works at Swindon. Houses, schools, shops and even medical facilities were provided and supported by the GWR, whilst the clubs, societies and events which sprang up under the auspices of the GWR were varied and numerous. This selection of photographs gives a small insight into the home and social lives of those who worked 'inside'.

A boarded-up shop, situated on the corner of Oxford Street and Emlyn Square, September 1929. The GWR notice fixed to the Oxford Street side of the building warns that 'Motor Lorries Must Not Enter This Street'. The Swindon Engineering Society occupied the building to the left, No.2 Emlyn Square.

A view of London Street, c.1915. The gas lamps and iron railings have long since gone. Behind the row of trees, which are also no longer there, runs the high brick wall enclosing the Carriage & Wagon Works. The imposing structure of the Mechanics Institute can be seen in the middle distance.

This photograph shows the back alley between two rows of cottages in the Railway Village. Although undated, the evidence of new extensions, outhouses and extensive renovations suggest this photograph was taken in the 1960s or '70s.

The dilapidated backyard of No.34 Faringdon Road. This photograph was taken prior to its renovation in the 1960s, when it was restored back to a 1900s railway worker's cottage to form a part of the adjacent GWR Museum.

Although there is no street name evident, the top of the Works water tower, which can be seen protruding above the roofs, suggests that this is a view of Bathampton Street. The evidence of television aerials dates this picture prior to the 1970s renovation of the Railway Village, when all modern fixtures that were considered to be out of keeping with the architecture of the buildings were removed.

A slightly blurred 1970s view of Exeter Street. A Courage Cockerel sign can be seen above the door of the Cricketers public house in the foreground of the picture, while a horse and rider are making their leisurely way down Exeter Street alongside the row of parked cars.

An impressive shot of the beautiful former residence of Chief Mechanical Engineer G.J. Churchward, looking, in this view, rather rundown and neglected. The reason this photograph of 'Newburn' in Dean Street was taken by the Drawing Office photographer in September 1936 was due to the fact that it was subsequently demolished to make way for a row of much less photogenic carriage sheds, which can be seen in chapter three.

In contrast to 'Newburn', the home of Chief Mechanical Engineer C.B. Collett in Church Place was far more modest. Legend has it that Collett was a very private individual; the high privet hedge surrounding the house seems to support this belief.

A view of the GWR Museum on Faringdon Road, a couple of years after it opened in 1962. The television aerial on the roof was installed for the benefit of the museum caretaker, who at that time lived on the premises.

When the walls of the GWR Museum were found to be moving during the 1970s, rescue work included inserting ties in the walls, re-roofing and general restoration. A large sign fixed to the scaffolding left passers-by in no doubt that the museum remained open for business as usual.

An aerial view taken in 1975, showing the Railway Village, the Carriage & Wagon Works and, beyond that, a rapidly developing Swindon.

This photograph of the Mechanics Institute Playhouse and Dance Hall was taken in July 1938, seven and a half years after the original theatre was ravaged by fire. The restored playhouse included the addition of a large brick fly tower from where the scenery was raised and lowered. The sign on the railings tells us that dances were held in the Dance Hall every Wednesday afternoon and Friday evening.

The swimming baths, which included Turkish and Russian baths, formed a part of the larger GWR Medical Fund building, which was based in Milton Road. The costume worn by the children posing for this photograph suggests it was taken pre-1914.

A 1908 view of the large swimming pool which was lavishly adorned with stained glass, colourful tiled walls, greenery and a first-floor viewing gallery. Although the pool was fitted with large gaslights, the majority of the time light filtered in through the large windows that ran along the length of the high arched roof.

A view of the smaller pool at the Medical Fund Swimming Baths. Many of the people in this photograph also appear in the previous view of the larger pool, suggesting that the two images were taken on the same day. All of the swimmers are young boys, some of whom are dressed in knee-length bathing suits.

The life span of Bristol Street School, shown here in the mid-1800s, was rather short. Built for the children of GWR workers in 1843-1844, and joined in 1857 by a separate infants school, the majority of the buildings were demolished in 1881 to make way for an ever-expanding Works. The infants school survived and was later converted into the Works laboratory.

A very crowded photograph of the annual GWR Fete at The Park. Although undated, the fashions suggest that this picture was taken around 1900. The fete was a hugely popular event. Everyone wore their Sunday best, and children were given a slice of fruitcake and tickets for two rides on the fairground, which can be seen in the background of this photograph.

Trip Fortnight was the main highlight of the GWR calendar, when Swindon all but shut down as its residents took their annual holiday. Pictured here in 1931, GWR workers and their families climb aboard the complimentary train that was to take them to their holiday in Weymouth, and a variety of other destinations.

Trip holidaymakers at Swindon Station, c.1910. This is a rare photograph in that it was unusual for 'Trip' trains to leave from the station. In order to cause minimum disruption to regular services, it was more the norm for these trains to be boarded from a variety of locations either inside the Works or further down the line.

The Reading Room in the Mechanics Institute, 1939. The reading bench that is 'Reserved For Ladies' is well stocked with home-style and fashion magazines, while more serious reading matter is available for the gentlemen. An austere ambience is created by the high ceiling, church-like windows, impressive gaslights and the likenesses of eminent engineers adorning the walls, including the busts of Daniel Gooch and Isambard Kingdom Brunel, which can be seen in the wide arched alcove towards the back of the photograph and are now on display at STEAM.

Opposite above: A view inside one of the wards of the GWR Hospital. Believed to have been taken between 1890 and 1900, this photograph, with the starched uniforms and the neatly laid dining table, show the formality of a Victorian hospital. A closer look shows the gentleman standing to the left of the mirror supporting himself on a pair of crutches.

Opposite below: A view of the Playhouse Theatre in the Mechanics Institute prior to the fire of 1930. The ornate plasterwork, carved balcony and leaded light windows made this a splendid place to see a performance. The well-padded benches at the front of the theatre were obviously reserved for the most important visitors.

The well-equipped GWR Fire Station. The fire engine in the centre of the picture is the Dennis Engine that was purchased for the station in 1912. To the right of the picture is the callboard which, when activated, summoned the firemen from their homes to duty. The roof space above the offices was utilised as a storeroom, which, when the station closed in 1986, still contained a number of parts for the 1912 Dennis Engine.

Fire Station staff in front of a 1942 fire engine, which is now preserved at the Science Museum at Wroughton. The GWR only had two fire engines – the 1912 and 1942 engines – during the life of the station, and were still using the 1942 engine when the Works finally closed.

The ladies of the Chief Mechanical Engineers Choir, photographed c.1930, with their Choir Master and an unknown gentleman.

A photograph of the GWR Rugby Team, c.1940. The dirty socks and dishevelled shirts suggest that this team had just played a match. Unfortunately, who the opposing team were and what the score was remain unknown.

The lady and gentlemen members of the GWR Harmonica Knights Band in 1936. As the name suggests, the main musical instrument performed on by the band was the harmonica.

Swindon GWR Accounts Staff Gleemen. This male voice choir were the winners of the GWR Musical Festival Silver Cup Trophy 1924-1928. Such was the quality and popularity of this group that they went on to record and release a number of 78rpm records.

A gathering of the Staff Association Veterans Choir on 25 May 1960. The choir are photographed proudly displaying a silver cup; unfortunately there is no mention on the reverse of the photograph what the cup was awarded for.

The very dapper-looking members of the Drawing Office Cricket Team, photographed c.1906.

98

Above: A photograph of the Great Western Silver Band taken outside the Mechanics Institute in 1925. Note the rich detail of the braiding on the uniforms. The gentleman in the front row with white gloves and baton is Conductor C. Baker.

Opposite above: An official photograph of the GWR Temperance Movement Orchestra taken *c*.1930. The secret of the elevated height of the fourth row is given away by the glimpse of the chairs that the gentlemen are standing on at either end of the row.

Opposite below: St John's Ambulance Association taking part in a display at Swindon Hospital, Saturday 17 June 1899. A large number of GWR staff joined the St John's Ambulance Association due to the number of accidents that occurred within the Works. Many of the men can be seen proudly wearing their St John's Ambulance Association badges and armbands.

A group of gentlemen from the Locomotive Managers Office suitably attired for their annual outing on 20 June 1914. A sobering thought is the fact that war broke out soon after this photograph was taken. How many of this group went off to fight and possibly never returned is something we are unlikely to find out.

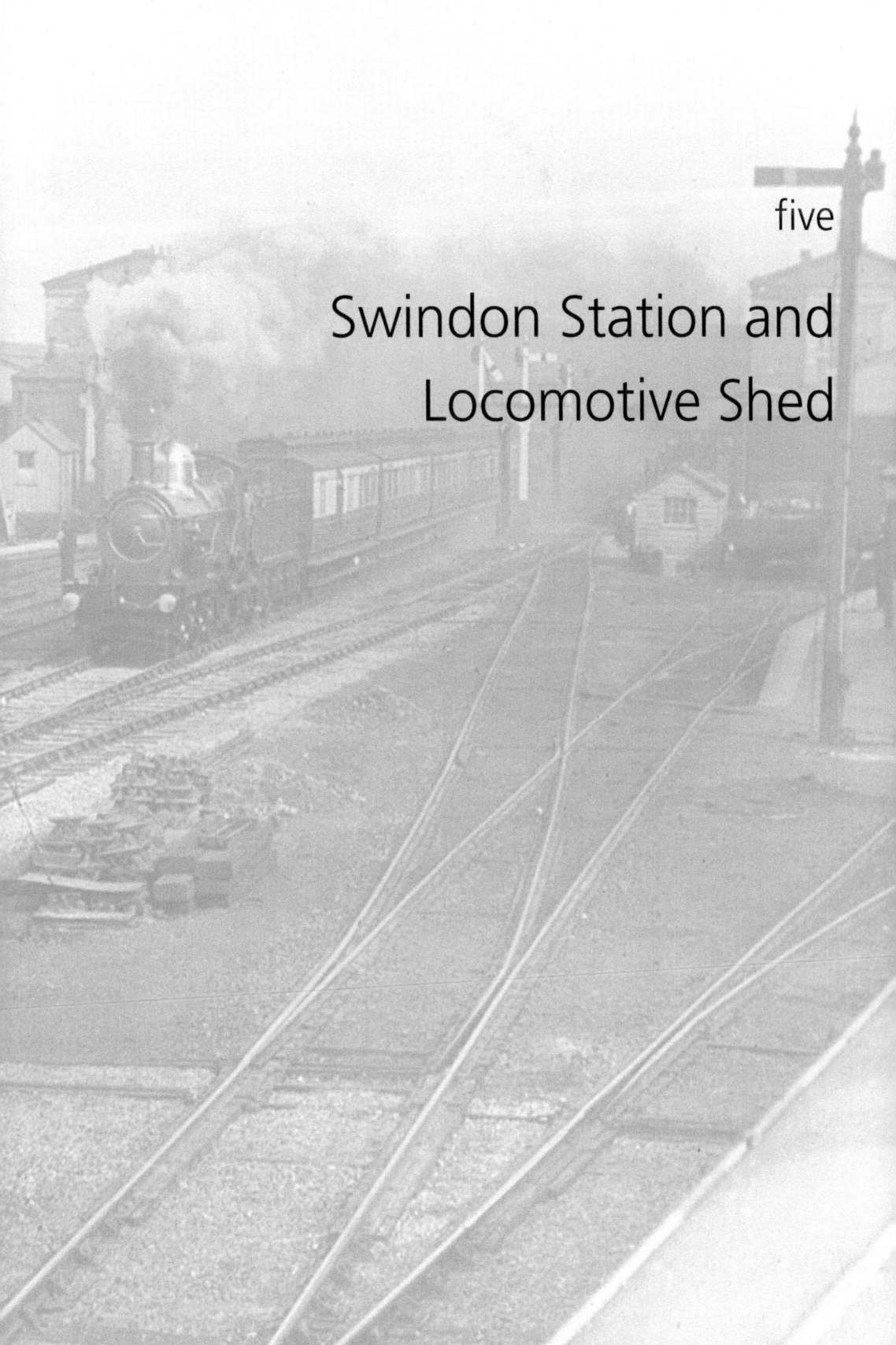

five

Swindon Station and Locomotive Shed

Swindon station opened for business in 1842, before the Railway Works were ready. A busy and thriving junction station, as well as receiving trains from Bristol and London, it also served as the destination for trains from the Highworth branch – opened in 1885 – and services on the Gloucester Line. In 1881 the rival Midland & South Western Junction Railway opened, and as a result the station was renamed Swindon Junction to prevent confusion with the M&SWJR station at Old Town. The old station buildings were demolished in the 1970s and replaced with a modern office block, and the station shrank to one large island platform. Today, however, the station is as busy as ever, and a new platform opened in the summer of 2003, to cope with extra business generated by an improved Bristol–London service.

Swindon does not now have a locomotive shed, largely a result of the huge changes in rolling stock, which means that few trains are now locomotive hauled. Photographs shown here, however, take us into the huge depot, which was formerly such a large part of the railway complex at Swindon.

There have been a number of views of the special occasion portrayed in this photograph. No doubt others were the result of the photographer who is patiently waiting next to the signal post in the foreground. The occasion was the running of the first non-stop express through the station, following the abolition of the ten-minute stop at Swindon in 1895. Before this date, the Great Western had been tied to an arrangement made in the 1840s whereby all trains to and from Bristol and London had to stop at Swindon to allow passengers to take refreshment in the refreshment rooms on the station.

The station forecourt in 1970, shortly before modernisation. For those interested in cars, there is an interesting selection of vehicles on view. As is the case at most stations, the 'No Parking' notices are being firmly ignored by those waiting for passengers from arriving trains. The taxi rank, complete with hut for taxi drivers, is situated close to the Queens Tap public house. Today taxis wait much nearer the station entrance.

The ticket office in January 1970, taken at a time when some modernisation had taken place, but many GWR features still remain, including the cast-iron 'In' and 'Out' signs on the wall and the ornate crush barriers close to each ticket window. The more modern enquiry office is a contrast to the peeling paint and general run-down air of the scene.

The run-down condition of the station is seen again in this photograph taken at the entrance to the stairs leading to the subway on 28 January 1970.

A much earlier photograph of one of the waiting rooms at Swindon Junction. The spartan feel to the room is not helped by the rather severe wooden benches and minimal decoration, which is confined to a number of framed cut-down British Railways posters. A coal-fired stove can be seen on the left of this 1950 picture.

Above: A final selection from the series of pictures taken prior to redevelopment. This image shows Platform 3 taken from the Reading end of the station. A number of the British Rail metal 'BRUTE' trolleys can be seen, full with mail sacks awaiting loading.

Right: A photograph from the collection of the late F.W. Hawksworth, the last Chief Mechanical Engineer at Swindon. It shows the scene at Swindon Junction on a sombre occasion – that of the run of the last steam hauled train on the Western Region – on 27 November 1965. As well as Hawksworth, the Mayor of Swindon, Councillor A.J.W. Dymond and Chief Locomotive Inspector Jack Hancock are also part of the crowd.

A William Hooper postcard showing GWR traffic department staff at Swindon, possibly before the departure of 'Trip' trains, although there is no indication on the card itself, which was posted in 1911. Third from the left is the Station Master at Swindon, John Brewer, whose picture was reproduced in the first volume of *Great Western Swindon*.

The first of a series of photographs showing trains around the station area features the futuristic Advanced Passenger Train on a test run through Swindon. The famous 'tilting train' was not a success, and did not progress beyond the experimental stage, becoming something of a joke amongst politicians, newspapermen and railway staff alike.

A GWR Hall Class locomotive No.6971 *Athelhampton Hall* on a fitted freight train passes Swindon in the early 1960s. Judging from its clean condition, the locomotive must have only recently been through the Works for overhaul.

A famous visitor to Swindon. Ex-LNER 4-6-2 *Mallard* draws in to the station past a King Class locomotive outside the Works in 1962. The locomotive was most famous for breaking the world speed record for steam locomotives in 1938 when it achieved 126mph. It is now the flagship locomotive for the National Railway Museum in York.

The reader might be somewhat mystified to see this photograph of what appears to be a train speeding through open countryside. This location, however, is Hay Lane Bridge, west of Swindon. The first station for Swindon was constructed by Brunel in the early 1840s close to this spot as a temporary stop for the town, until the proper station was completed in 1842. There is no indication today that there was ever any structure on the site, and certainly none is visible in this picture of the Bristol Pullman speeding past on 9 January 1962.

The interior of the roundhouse at Swindon Locomotive Shed in April 1962. All the locomotives seen in this photograph are examples of tank engines, the largest being a 72xx 2-8-2 locomotive No.7226 built at the Works in 1935.

A group of locomotives outside the large shed complex in May 1962. Identifiable are 4-6-0's No.6967 *Willesley Hall*, No.4956 *Plowden Hall* and No.7011 *Banbury Castle*.

A fine individual portrait by Jim Russell of GWR 4-6-0 No.5002 *Ludlow Castle* outside the shed in April 1962.

Above left: Driver W.J. Hall on the footplate of 4-6-0 No.4098 *Kidwelly Castle*, pictured at Swindon on 11 June 1958.

Above right: A photograph of Driver Low, full of detail for those interested in railway uniform and costume, taken at Swindon in 1947. He has placed elastic or string around the bottom of his trousers to prevent soot and dirt ruining the clothes underneath, and is holding a large piece of cotton waste, very necessary whilst oiling the locomotive, which can be identified as No.5067 *St Fagans Castle*.

Every shed had a Mutual Improvement class, which ensured that staff were trained in the art and science of caring for, driving and firing steam locomotives. This group photograph taken in 1911 also shows a famous face in the centre, that of W.A. Stanier who, after a career at Swindon, was later to become Chief Mechanical Engineer of the London Midland & Scottish Railway.

six

Swindon Products: Some GWR Locomotives

There have already been many books and articles illustrating the huge variety of locomotives built and maintained at Swindon Works in the steam era. The authors have picked out a number of interesting and historic images from the museum's collection, although this is by no means a representative selection!

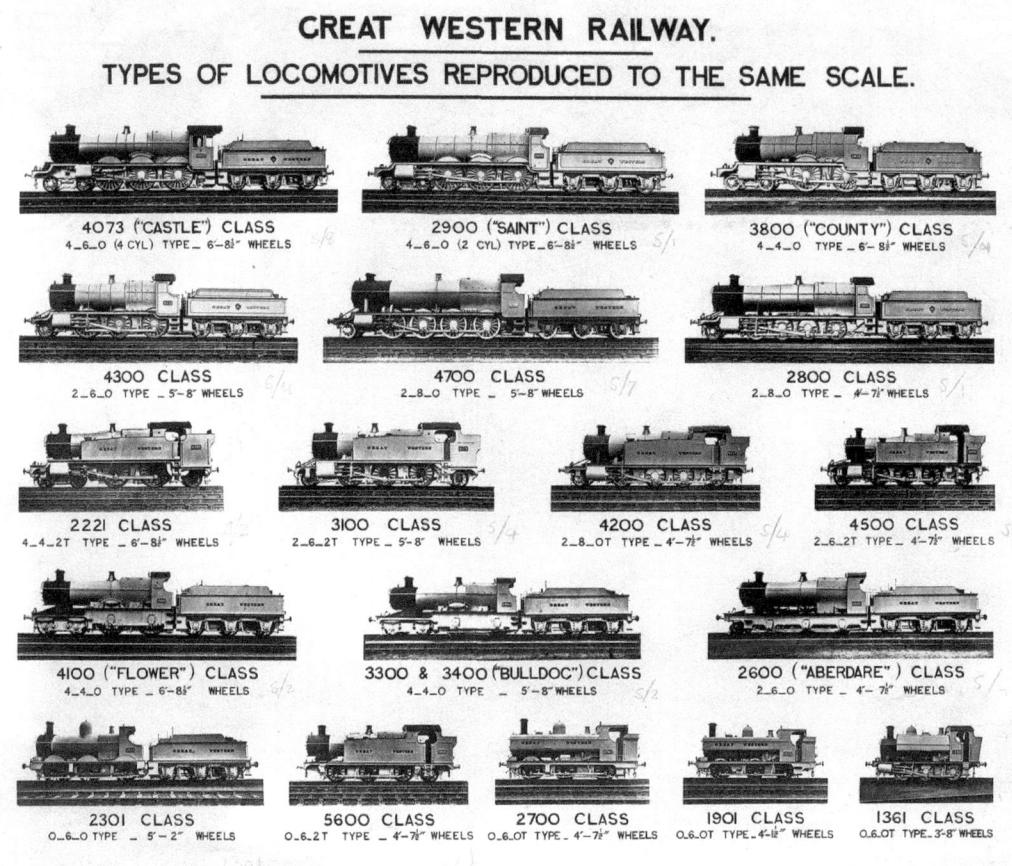

A composite photograph used by the Great Western in many of its publications to illustrate the different types of engines it operated, from large express types, to small tank locomotives. This example must date from after 1923 when the Castle Class was introduced, and before 1927, as the King Class has yet to make an appearance.

Opposite top: A marvellous photograph of the premier locomotives to run on the broad gauge. Nominally a rebuild of the Iron Duke Class, these Rover Class 4-2-2s hauled expresses from London to Bristol at high speed, and illustrate the ultimate in broad gauge power. Bulkeley was constructed at Swindon in 1880 and withdrawn in May 1892.

Opposite below: The crew of 0-6-0 1661 class saddle tank No.1691 pose for the camera. There is much detail in the picture, including the re-railing jack fixed to the footplate of the engine at the front end, and the driver's oil can clipped to the side plates of the cab. This locomotive was built in 1887 and finally scrapped in 1927.

The driver of 2-6-0 Aberdare Class locomotive No.2641 has oil can and rag in hand, whilst his fireman remains on the cab. Both have been hard at work since the engine is spotless, although close examination of the tender shows that the coal does not look of the highest quality.

The reason for this group photograph in front of Swindon-built 2-6-2 locomotive No.3141 is not known. The locomotive was built in 1906 and withdrawn in 1952.

A view taken at Westbourne Park before the Great War of one of the most famous Great Western locomotives, 4-4-0 No.3440 *City of Truro*. In 1903 the engine became the first to break the 100mph barrier. The locomotive was later preserved at Swindon, and two pictures of the engine are to be seen in chapter seven. The engine is due to be returned to steam for the centenary of its record-breaking exploits in 2004.

The ubiquitous Hall Class locomotives designed by C.B. Collett were built in great numbers, and ran all over the Great Western system. This example, No.4919 *Dartington Hall* was one of the first batch of engines built in 1929, and is seen here on an up Swansea express near Reading in the early 1960s.

In the same location as *Dartington Hall*, Jim Russell has photographed another Collett design, the Castle Class. This example is No.7005 *Sir Edward Elgar* originally named *Lamphey Castle*, and renamed in honour of the British composer in 1957.

Although there are pictures of the most famous example of the King Class locomotive No.6000 *King George V* elsewhere in the book, this photograph is of another of the class, No.6018 *King Henry VI*, built at Swindon in 1928. What is also of note in this picture is the enormous stack of coal behind the engine on the coal stage of the unidentified depot. Nevertheless, the sheer size and power suggested by the locomotive design are hard to ignore in this 1936 photograph.

seven

Great Western Preserved

Since this book consists of images from the collections of STEAM: Museum of the Great Western Railway, it seemed apt to include a number of pictures of the larger exhibits from the collection, some before preservation, and a number showing the move of items from the old Faringdon Road building to our new premises.

Above: A photograph taken in the Works in 1925 shortly before the completion of the replica locomotive *North Star*. The original broad gauge engine of the same name had been kept at the Works from 1870 when it had been withdrawn, until 1906 when, after being offered to various institutions including the Science Museum without success, it was scrapped, along with another broad gauge survivor, *Lord of the Isles*. The replica was constructed initially to provide a major exhibit for the Stockton & Darlington Railway centenary exhibition at Faverdale in 1925, although it was also shipped to the United States with *King George V* in 1927.

Left: Although another photograph of the *North Star* outside the Town Hall in 1950 was reproduced in the previous volume, the authors felt that this marvellous print of a family proudly standing in front of the engine was worthy of inclusion. It would be interesting to know if the family had a railway connection; given the number of railway staff still employed at this time, this is more than likely!

The record-breaking 4-4-0 locomotive *City of Truro* being manoeuvred into place before being installed in the old GWR Museum in Faringdon Road in April 1962. Note the metal plates laid to protect the pavement, and the solid tyres of the Pickfords trailer unit used to move the locomotive from the Works to the museum.

The scene outside the museum some twenty-two years later in 1984, when the *City of Truro* was removed from the museum to be restored and returned to steam for the GWR's 150th anniversary celebrations the following year. The engine was removed in an overnight operation, which also saw its replacement with GWR Diesel Railcar No.4 the following night.

A fine picture of the GWR's flagship locomotive No.6000 *King George V* not long after construction in 1927. What is of most interest is the location of the picture, for it was taken at Baltimore Yard on the engine's trip to the United States as the guest of the Baltimore & Ohio Railway, which was celebrating its centenary that year. To allow the engine to run on American railways, it was fitted with a Westinghouse braking system, which can be seen on the side of the locomotive smokebox.

An unknown photographer has captured this moody image of *King George V* at rest at Old Common Locomotive Shed in March 1962. The brass bell, presented to the Great Western by the Baltimore & Ohio Railway after its trip, gleams in the gloom of the depot.

The group assembled here were inspecting a special casting made to be fixed to the side of *King George V* during a celebratory run in 1974, to mark the mark the end of the borough of Swindon and its replacement by Thamesdown Borough Council. The engine had not long been returned to steam through the sponsorship of the Hereford cider company, H.P. Bulmer. Sir Peter Prior, the leading light in returning the engine to steam is pictured here with (left to right) Harry Roberts, the Swindon Works Manager, Peter Wicks, Fred Knowles and Bernard Staite.

A Jim Russell photograph of two locomotives which were a key part of the old GWR Museum displays. The main subject of the picture is the 4-6-0 Star Class locomotive *Lode Star* which had been withdrawn in the 1950s, but retained for preservation, as had the diminutive 0-6-0 Dean Goods engine No.2516 stabled behind it. The latter engine is now on display at STEAM: Museum of the Great Western Railway, but *Lode Star* is now exhibited at the National Railway Museum at York. Both are pictured in July 1961, having been overhauled at the Works, ready for movement to the museum, which was due to open the following year.

The end of the line at Faringdon Road as 0-6-0 Pannier Tank locomotive No.9400 is made ready to leave the building for the last time in February 2000. The old museum closed to the public in October 1999, after thirty-seven years of service, and over two weekends, all the large exhibits were moved by road to their new home at STEAM: Museum of the Great Western Railway, back on the Railway Works site.

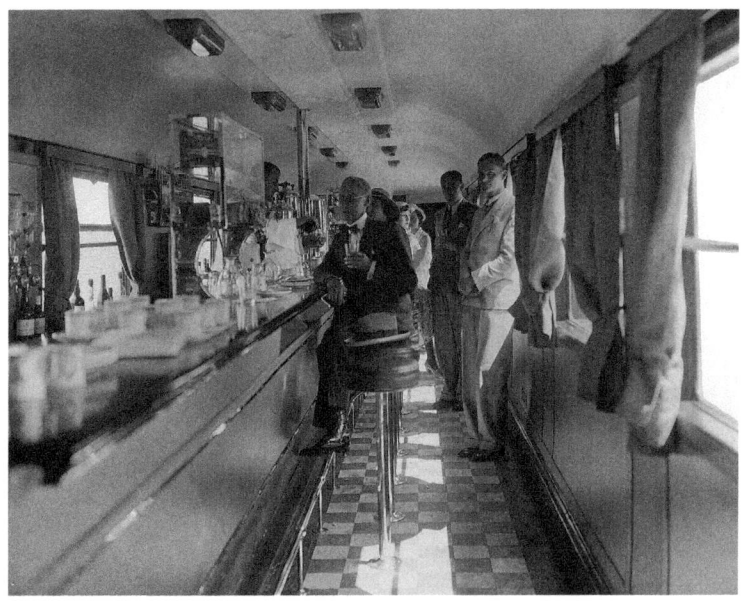

To end this section, a publicity photograph of one of the museum's carriages. Great Western Railway *Quicksnack* buffet car No.9631 was originally built as an alternative to the more formal restaurant cars, and was used by the company on its express services. Fitted with a long bar which ran the length of the carriage, this view taken in 1938 is full of Art Deco period detail.

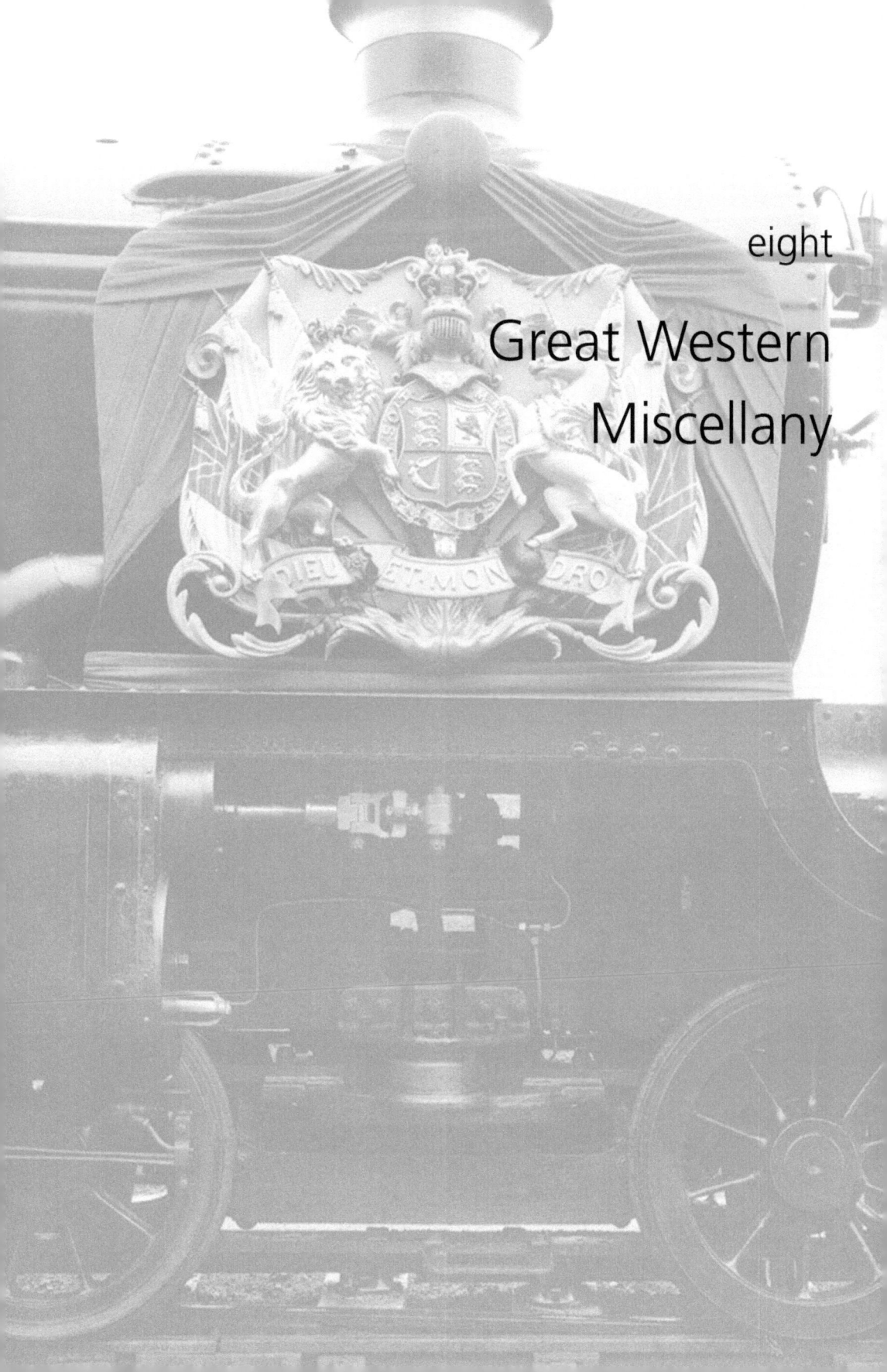

eight

Great Western Miscellany

In a large photographic collection, there are often many images which sometimes defy exact categorisation. This chapter includes images of this type, along with others, which for no better reason, caught the eye of the compilers, and were thought worthy of inclusion!

Above: A view of an early 0-4-0 petrol electric diesel, purchased by the GWR from the Fowler Co. of Leeds in 1933. It worked at Swindon until 1940, when it was sold to Cohen & Son's of Leeds.

Left: A Drawing Office photograph of the fixing of the Royal Coat of Arms for the funeral train of *King George V* in 1936. The two cast-iron coats of arms are still part of the museum's collection, and their enormous weight must have had at least some effect on the performance of the locomotive.

Right: The first of two photographs taken during the visit of Princess Elizabeth to the Works on 15 November 1950. The future Queen is seen unveiling the nameplate of No.7037 *Swindon*, the last GWR design locomotive to be built at the Works.

Below: Following in the footsteps of the previous Royal Visit to the Works in 1924, the Princess Royal was taken to the Foundry, where a special casting commemorating her visit was made. Both this casting and the one manufactured for the visit of King George and Queen Mary are still preserved at Swindon, although not currently on public display.

The scene at a ceremony held to mark the centenary of the birth of the GWR's most influential locomotive engineer, George Jackson Churchward, on 31 January 1957. Paying their respects at the grave of Churchward are (left to right): the Swindon Town Clerk (not named), R.A. Smeddle, F.C. Hall, F.W. Hawksworth, C.T. Roberts, Canon Thomas Godsell, and the Mayor of Swindon, N. Toye.

The Mayor's Chamber at the Civic Offices in Swindon was the scene for this photograph of Mayor A.W.J Dymond, R.F. Hanks, and F.W. Hawksworth. The Mayor and Hawksworth were of course GWR stalwarts, and R.F. Hanks was the head of British Railways (Western Region) at the time. Also of note in this 1966 view is the model on the small table in front of the group, which was presented to the Borough of Swindon on the occasion of the opening of the GWR Museum in 1962.

Right: The search for an adequate water supply for the Works at Swindon was one which took up a great deal of time and resources for the GWR. Eventually, the company was able to obtain a good source of water from a well sunk at Kemble, some miles north of the town. This photograph taken in 1968 shows work taking place at the site, close to the station.

Below: A general view of Kemble Station, before the closure of the Tetbury and Cirencester branch lines, for which passengers changed at the station. On the right of the picture is one of the experimental diesel units used on the Cirencester branch for some months. Despite the closure of both branches, the station is still a busy location, and has a high number of passengers who commute to London each day from their homes in the Cotswold area.

To conclude this selection of photographs, it is fitting to include a portrait of the nameplate of Castle Class engine No.5069 *Isambard Kingdom Brunel*, taken in the scrap yard at Swindon in May 1962. Although the locomotive was broken up, the plate remains, and it reminds us of the contribution of perhaps the world's most famous engineer, Brunel, who created the railway and works that have been so vividly brought to life in this collection.